To My Grandmothers

NINO GUGUNISHVILI

You Will Have a Black Labrador

This book was professionally typeset on Reedsy.
Find out more at reedsy.com

Contents

In Search of Peter   1

A Long Story of a Short Hair   5

A Family Album   11

Make Me an Omelette   15

Till Death Do Us Part   20

A Letter to My Unborn Children   25

A Belated Apology to My Dog   29

Dembe   32

Ara Means No! Or, the Art of Saying No   37

Do You Speak English?   39

Notes   43

About the Author   44

Also by Nino Gugunishvili   45

In Search of Peter

I n between eating quinoa and goat cheese salads, the decision was made. We had to search for Peter. We became fiercely determined to not just search for Peter, but to find him.

A handsome guy, tall, possibly dark blond, blue eyed, just the right amount of funky and sophisticated, in his early forties, an entrepreneur, a digital prodigy, a start-upper, but not the nerdy type, no, a very easygoing one and fun to be around, not just for me, for my girlfriends included. He'd be generous and would invite us to many social outings, not that I care about social outings much, I'd be okay to snuggle on a couch with him (but I'm not telling Margot the 'couch snuggling' part, because she's all about dragging out my socialite side). So, we move the story further, exploring going-outs in Peter's company to the art galleries, movies, and all the trendiest restaurants in town. Peter's family is from Boston and nowhere else, since Boston, we were told, is all about old money and wealth, but Peter doesn't really need one.

'Where does he live?' Margot asks me, but we both know the answer without saying it out loud. Upper Manhattan or Soho is where Peter's apartment is, all Scandinavian style, beige, wood floors, and minimalistic design. I can almost see him, in the morning, barefoot, wearing jeans and a T-shirt, drinking his coffee in that George Clooney Nespresso commercial style, then checking his email casually and leaving for work to his office, or maybe he doesn't have an office and works from home, you know. He's cool and relaxed, most of the time, and he's only just a bit annoyed because I'm choosing one and the same place for our summer getaways, which is the south of France, of course. Not that he has anything against the south of France; he only reminds me, gently, that there are many other beautiful places scattered around the globe, and why don't we go to Positano, Italy, next time? Positano it is, I agree, ignoring that nagging feeling inside me, rising.

We arrive at Positano, living in a little family-type hotel, run by a couple, Lucia and Salvatore. Lucia spoils us rotten with her mouthwatering pastas, lasagnes, and raviolis, and Salvatore brings his son's artisan wines to the table and fills our glasses, and we're drinking, and then sitting outside on a patio and watching the sunset from the cliff and kissing and later making love upstairs and laughing, and I tell Peter it's so great we came to Positano and I kiss him fondly. I continue kissing him every now and then for the next couple of days, until Lucia introduces me to her son Gianni over the dinner, and I can't take my eyes off his tanned muscular hands. When he starts speaking in that sexiest of accents, I'm dumbstruck and I lie about having a headache and Gianni drives me to the pharmacy in the middle of the night, and we have amazing sex in his car. By the time I wake up in Gianni's bed the next morning, Peter is gone. I feel guilty over breakfast. I stay with Gianni in Positano till the end of the summer. We're off to Naples, and Venice, and Florence in September; by the time we reach Rome, I can understand enough Italian to find out that Gianni's engaged to the love of

2

his life, a dark-haired, green-eyed beauty, Laura, who bursts into Gianni's apartment one evening—and stays.

I leave for New York. I stumble on Peter's photo on Facebook. He's now working in Hong Kong, with Sui, his fiancé, and their cat, whose name I don't remember, and I can't ask since Peter has blocked me from everywhere. Why do I care?—asks Tom, a freelance writer, and a college professor, as I make him spaghetti, by Lucia's recipe, but it's never as good as hers. Tom's obsessed with shoe polish. I like his slightly grim poems and short stories. He doesn't mind my second chin. The lack of sex is compensated for by talks about literature. I masterfully hide my love for chick lit, romance, and Scandinavian thrillers. He dumps me for Suzanne at a writing retreat and claims she's his muse for the rest of his life.

I buy a bottle of Pinot Grigio to celebrate, inviting my next-door neighbour, David, over. David is a busy surgeon, so we meet only occasionally, between his hospital shifts. He's not at all like my favourite doctor from a TV show; he has no idea about my favourite TV show, and when I point that out, he says I'm delusional. I take it as an insult and change apartment.

My new job offer sends me to Stockholm, and to a three-month encounter with a young, immature Thorsten, a computer geek, shocked by my lack of computer skills and love for scented candles. I'm in awe of his father's comics collection, and a super-comfortable couch on which we have a brief interlude. Thorsten tells me he's heartbroken, writes a song and a lengthy post underneath, calling me bitch, and gets several likes and shares from Peter—and Gianni and Tom and David—along with a contract from one of the recording studios. I send his father a drawing of a Spiderman with a huge penis from the Stockholm airport. He never replies.

3

'Enough!' Margot screams, gulping the last of the Chardonnay. 'Poor Peter, it was supposed to be his story, and I was going to visit you, and we'd have so much fun, and now it's a bit sad that you never stayed together, even if we invented the whole thing over a salad,' she tells me.

'In fact, we came up with Peter's story either at Prince Street or at Bleaker Street, if we're following the actual facts,' I reply and follow her gaze.

She whispers, 'Please, try not to stare, but that guy sitting two tables ahead might look exactly like...'

'Oh, great, I might now have to edit the story!' I say, turn my head, and gasp.

A Long Story of a Short Hair

My hair took a stellar revenge on me! My hair betrayed me this last Tuesday. I saw it very clearly in my bedroom mirror; that white, hairless spot on the left side of my scalp as an unwanted, unexpected evidence of my age, telling me outright and plain that I was no longer twenty and I was no longer thirty as well. It also indicated that I sacrificed my hair to my obsession with cinema and romantic comedies in particular. I looked at my reflection in the mirror in horror, and while I stared in disbelief, a smell of a burned hair came in, bringing back the memory of my eighth or ninth grade visit to a hairdresser who made me my first-ever perm.

All of my friends' mothers I knew, my mother included, loved a popular French singer, and ultimately her haircut. The same one I have, in almost all of the photos from my childhood: holding a baby doll, dressed in a white turtleneck underneath a dark blue velvet dress, and wearing a bob. Who would dare object if you were taken to the best hairdresser in town? My mother insisted that her hairdresser Liza was the best.

Mom found Liza when she was in her twenties, and never thought of changing to anyone else, until Liza died. In a Soviet-era Tbilisi, it wasn't easy to find a hair stylist who'd make you look like a foreign movie star. You'd more easily travel to a non-

5

communist part of the world than find a good hairdresser in town, and if you did, you didn't tell anyone. You'd eagerly share food recipes or new books, but a good hairdresser's contact details? Never! *Omertà!*

When I firmly expressed my wish to curl my seemingly long hair, Liza was the only one to be trusted. I remember sitting under a huge, grey hair dryer, waiting for my new curls to finally form, and a smell of a burned, damaged hair that followed me everywhere, for the whole six months afterwards. It was one of my first independent decisions regarding my looks, and as it turns out twenty-five years later, not the smartest one. As a child and as a teenager I wasn't much interested in what I wore or how my hair looked. The saying I heard from someone's grandmother, passed from generation to generation, insisting that a woman is only as good as her hair is, didn't resonate with me at all. Not then, not ever. Truth be told, none of my acquaintances ever met that mythical grandmother. I wonder what kind of hair she had that boosted her self-confidence so much?

I wasn't a tomboy but I wasn't a girl loving to dress up, or put makeup on, either. 'Whenever they address you, they say "mademoiselle" and we're always referred as madames!' my friend told me once. 'You don't have any wrinkles at all,' another one continued. I should send them the photo of my hairless scalp, to never worry about the unfairness of life again. Bitches! Truth be told, they had a point. I always (well, up to this Tuesday morning) looked younger than my actual age. I was used to people being shocked when I told them how old I really was. 'Unbelievable!' they would exclaim. 'We're so jealous of your genes!' they'd say. Genes? My dad lost all of his hair before I met him, before he became my dad, and my mom's hair turned almost grey in her last year of school, which she turned into advantage, cutting it short and chic. Physical appearance was never an important part of my self-identification, much to the dismay of my mother.

'You have to trim your brows! Are you going out with that hair?' She'd freeze in horror looking at me. 'That hair' meant it wasn't properly combed and it was far below her standards and understanding. Easy for her to say, wearing a short haircut almost all of her life, versus my brown, thick, unruly long haircuts, bobs, perms, highlights, and bobs and bobs and bobs of different colours all over again. Sometimes those experiments were on the verge of radical; I cut my hair too short, or dyed it with unidentified colour, or let it grow until it was long enough to cover all my back. Still, it always was just hair that needed to be taken care of, from time to time—that said, not very often, in fact, very rarely.

As I grew older, I developed an idiosyncrasy about beauty salons in general. While seated in an armchair, waiting for a hairdresser to colour, cut, or style my hair, I realised with a painful clarity what a waste of my precious time it was. I felt I could be doing things much more important than exchanging pleasantries with my hair master, and on more than several occasions I wanted to run away, with my hair still wet and unwashed, but I surrendered and stayed, which pissed me off even more. I hated that feeling of a time that froze, the implication that a woman was to enjoy these beauty procedures; that an hour spent at a beauty salon was a time to legally relax and socialize. I hated that kingdom of nail polishes, manicures and pedicures, comfortable chairs and freshly brewed coffees where nothing mattered except the length and colour of your hair and nails and the thickness and shape of your eyebrows.

Strangely, though, the more I hated beauty salons, the more hair stylists loved me. I never complained; whatever they did, it was fine with me. I barely talked, secretly counting minutes to get the hell out of there. I was an obedient client, an obedient child, and a non-rebellious teenager.

Then, at the age of twenty-four, I fell in love...with a haircut. Almost all of my friends immediately felt the same and all of us frantically wanted the same hair style as the heroine in the movie *French Kiss*. We learned those movie lines by heart, we collectively dreamed of travelling to Paris and then to the south of France, tasting French cheese and staying there, falling madly in love, but we got obsessed with the haircut in the first place. From then on, any hair stylist who'd make even something slightly similar to that haircut was proclaimed a master of our universe with a capital M, not that there were many. The movie itself became a turning point, or as we would now call it a trend, the word we didn't have in our vocabulary back then. We stormed into beauty salons with a fierce determination to get *that haircut.* We brought the photos, we kept explaining, fully using our body language, and all the presentation and expression skills we had. Some of us got lucky, but not entirely. It was never exactly the same. Almost there, yet not perfect, with some elements missing, either the colour or the length. But we needed that fresh-out-of-bed look so badly! We believed it was more than just a haircut. It symbolized novelty, adventure, arriving at the point of your life when you were ready to go, to leave, to travel and explore, to feel independent! It meant that something as romantic and as thrilling as *French Kiss* might happen to us too, and in order for those cinematic dreams to materialize, all we needed was that haircut. Through our very first jobs, lovers, heartbreaks, and evolving new friendships, divorces and new marriages, that haircut stayed with us as sign that no matter where we were, we'd always agree on one thing: that haircut was perfect. It was timeless.

However, in all that collective admiration, I considered myself the most in love with it. I was the one I thought needed that particular hairstyle the most, contrary to the opinions of my hairstylists. For several years I tried to get it, but the harder I tried, the more I failed. My hair meanwhile changed its length and colour and structure; and, tired of the many unsuccessful attempts, I finally gave up—until the movie *You've Got Mail* came out and I re-fell in love with a slightly changed hairstyle of the main heroine all over again.

This time, it turned out, I was alone. My friends seemed well past the point of fantasizing about it. Single and married, they found other things to deal with in their late twenties.

I now had an undivided love that I could cherish uninterrupted. Once again, that short blond hair showed that a true romance was possible! Who cared that it was just a movie? Who cared that it was a fictionalized world? Who cared when there was New York, and Central Park, and a golden retriever? Finally I got a very short something commonly called a 'boyish style' in which I resembled Harry Potter if he'd turn twenty-seven. I kept trying mercilessly. I didn't know that soon there would be a whole revolution coming, called *Sex and the City*, taking our lives by storm, by an avalanche, turning everything we thought we knew about sex, romance, breakups, friendships, and life upside down. And just as when you fell in love for the second time, rediscovering the sharpness and the depth of your feelings flooding through you, I temporarily forgot about the movies I adored. There were only four women I wanted to watch and listen to, the heroines of the *Sex and the City*. It was an awakening

9

to fashion and glamour and love and to Mr. Big, whom we loved and hated and then loved again, along with Carrie Bradshaw. I remember how jealous I felt when one of my closest friends flew to New York. Not only had she a glamorous job, she was also secretly watching *Sex and the City* every morning, on her coffee breaks!

It finally hit me that there was so much more to feel and explore, that there were places we had to visit, food we had to taste, people we had to meet and possibly fall in and out of love with, an understanding of the fact that even if I turned into an old lady with my head turning completely bald, I could always wear a cool collection of wigs, couldn't I?

By the way, I recently discovered a lovely shop on the Upper East Side of New York, with wigs in all shapes, colours, and forms. Do you need the exact address?

A Family Album

There is something out-fashioned, old, yet very real in the old family photos. The way we pose and smile, the way we sit or stand or what we wear. The way in which it seems we know something very important is happening right in that moment of our lives. These photos, capturing our childhoods, our stepping into adulthood, or showing us on our family vacations, on weddings, birthdays, or catching us at simple, everyday moments of our lives, those photos in the frames on the shelves are holding something more intangible, difficult to name, a story. Taking a photo was an event you had to prepare for, putting your fancy clothes on, prepping your hair, and then a photographer would come for a photo shoot and then you'd pose, and giggle and dance around. Oh, and the Polaroids? That joy of seeing the images slowly forming, first the colours intensifying, then the silhouettes and objects, and finally faces! That surprise and the excitement to see what was in there, while you waited for the image to finally dry!

That girl, with big, round glasses in a red jumper hugging her mom, smiling at the camera, is that me? It's Paris, 1994; we were in a fancy seafood restaurant. My glasses are awful, magnifying my thick, not yet trimmed eyebrows. My mom looks young and happy, though. She's much younger than I am right now.

Our study is full with bookshelves and bookshelves are over-loaded with family photos. Coloured, black and white, old and most recent...

From the number of those images displayed you wouldn't think I have developed a photo phobia. I'm there, my story too vulnerably exposed behind those glassed shelves, next to my parents, my brother's, two of my nephews, my sister-in-law, and of course my dog. I seem to be the happiest in the photos taken with my dog, wearing a huge dark green parka with a hoodie, jeans and dirty boots, since it's winter and we're returning from a long morning walk. My dog is also dressed in his blue winter coat, his ears wet from snow. I can almost smell those wet, fluffy dog ears.

Next photo is of my nephew Nick. He's probably six or seven there, ready to hit the soccer ball. He's too focused, very much in the moment, concentrated, his little hand in the air. Next, there's a photo of my mom and dad together; they're posing in a museum, I can see a Venus statue behind. Contrary to me, my parents always brought photos from whatever places they travelled to. For them, photos were prolongation of their memories, justifying that yes, those moments of happiness, of enjoying life and each other's company, existed. Next photo is from my brother's wedding. He looks young, a little too young to be called a husband, but back then, some twenty years ago, I didn't think so. I was waiting for a huge party!

His elder son's photo, looking directly into the camera, running, is the next one on the shelf. I guess it's a picture from his schooldays; he looks almost exactly like me, on the photo from the right, where I have a very short haircut and round glasses again, fresh out of school, before entering university. I have a frightened look on my face. Serious but frightened. In another image from when I was in third or fourth grade, I'm at school, math lesson. I remember clearly that we had a math test that day, for which I was unprepared, and then a photographer from a local newspaper came to the classroom. I have no idea why he chose me for his story. Probably because of that look at my face; sad, melancholic, and fed up with the classes. In one of the other photos also from school, I'm the only one wearing the black school uniform, when all the other girls are dressed in white. Of course, I didn't pay attention to my teacher asking us to wear the white one and she yelled at me the next day, saying that I'm flying in the clouds as always!

The next photo I glance at is one of my favourites. There are five of us, at my grandma's house: me, my mom, my brother, my aunt, and my cousin. We're sitting at the table, dining. We're not looking into the camera. We don't even notice that there's someone, probably my dad, taking the picture. It looks pastoral and happy. I miss that house, and all of us there.

My eyes dart from one photo to another, all our life is there, ripped open, bare, exposed, telling a story of several generations from one family.

There are my grandparents on their wedding day, then there's a photo of my father and me. I'm holding a pipe and we're laughing. Me again, alone, standing by the wall, in a red dress. Sometimes I wonder...how much of that girl in white school uniform happy that a newspaper reporter ruined her exam—or the other one, laughing with her dad—is still me. Is she still alive?

In between those images on the shelf, there's a book that my mom proudly put in the front row. There's a girl with a suitcase on its cover, a short author biography on its back, a book blurb, and no author photo of mine.

Make Me an Omelette

[1]For my first-ever cooking fiasco, I blame my brother and the day he asked me to make two boiled eggs. I threw myself into the task unaware of the consequences it would have on my life.

'Don't forget to salt them, okay?' he told me nonchalantly, and that detail of adding salt completely ruined my teenager years. The dish I prepared after an hour of struggle resembled boiled eggs like a giraffe resembles a cat. I had no idea how to boil and salt the eggs simultaneously, so I decided to simply smash them into the hot water. By the end of my first-ever culinary attempt, we had no more eggs in the house and I had to clean every surface in our kitchen, accompanied by my brother's hysterical laughter.

This story became an anecdote. My family members would tell it over and over to their friends and to friends of friends. It mercilessly followed me everywhere I went, and resurfaced when I least expected it. Two boiled eggs—the embarrassment of my life.

That's why, from the age of eleven or twelve, I was willing to have a go at any new challenge except, well, cooking. But—I have to add a huge *but* here—in my family, cooking and serving a meal always was, and still is, quintessential. The most important question you'd hear at our house is either 'Are you hungry?' or 'Have you eaten?' presuming that as long as you were not hungry, everything else was secondary. A good meal, according to our family philosophy, could defeat any drama, any worry, any existential crisis. Everything could be resolved once you'd shared a meal with your family or friends.

With culinary skills, you could fear nothing, you could win any battle. Cold dishes, hot dishes, starters, side dishes, main dishes, desserts, you had to master them all and then, on most occasions, feed at least twenty guests effortlessly. No woman in our family bragged about it. The ability to cook was never considered anything extraordinary. Rather, it was an intuitive talent that would eventually blossom as you matured and started your own family. Tables loaded with traditional Georgian food and wine, of course, were seen as standard, and every girl was expected to continue the tradition. Good cooking was synonymous with happiness, prosperity, kindness, and with the homes where grandmothers were reigning chefs preparing Satsivis, Khachapuris, and Gozinakis for the New Year, and mothers were sous chefs who made desserts, tarts, and pies, and decorated tables. Cooking was a bond between generations.

My grandmother's masterpiece was Khinkali, a dish originating from the mountainous regions of Georgia. My mother's all-time special was a creamy dessert called Ideal. Although I've never seen my other grandmother in the actual process of cooking, she knew everything about making a perfect fish dish, as her family came from one of the seaside towns. But it was her sister who was the undisputed queen of their kitchen. At any part of the day, she always had something yummy for you.

It didn't take me long to discover that I was a complete outsider. The boiled eggs disaster shut the kitchen door for me. My family members gently hinted I was not expected to be responsible for feeding our family. My conformist self chose the best possible way of coexistence, and I became an observer, a taster, an eater, but never a maker of food. As much as I loved dining out, or trying new cuisines when travelling, the creative part of preparing a dish was never what I was drawn to. I find movies, books, fashion, TV way more thrilling than eating, let alone cooking. I never saw life through the scope of delightful dining experiences.

As we grew up, my friends married, became mothers and wives and started cooking independently, rigorously throwing themselves into culinary adventures. Most of the time, I was there to taste, observing their evolution. Chicken soups for their toddlers were an epitome of the early stages of marriage, followed by Caesar salads and pizzas, rice puddings, barbe-cues, and pastas, fried turkey and foie gras, and guacamoles, which took our friendships through divorces, new husbands, our children becoming teenagers, new lovers, and successful careers. Dishes became milestones that signalled new turns, highlighting changes in tastes and priorities.

In my own life trajectory, eating and having basic cooking skills remained a low priority until the day I fell madly in love. Bernard worked in a less than fancy French restaurant in Vichy, France, where I was spending a month studying French. On our second meeting, Bernard suggested that the fastest way to learn a foreign language was through making love. While I can't exactly recall my French improving that summer, I remember how unbelievably delicious Bernard's omelettes were; so soft, crunchy, yummy, yellow and warm, and sunny. I devoured every bite. Bernard enlightened me to the thrill of watching someone cooking just for you, especially if you were head over heels with that someone. Bernard made exquisite apple tarts too. But for me, he'll forever be king of the morning-after-sex omelettes.

We split two days before my departure, and I never heard from Bernard again. Strangely, though, meeting him in my early twenties left me forever attached to men who were exceptionally good at making omelettes, or eggs Benedict—any dish, in fact, that had eggs as an essential ingredient.

Sebastian, a tanned surfer I met at the Istanbul airport as our flight to Tbilisi was delayed, had long muscular hands, and a curly ponytail, swinging on my nose as we woke up in my apartment two days later. Sebastian went to the kitchen to make…yes, an omelette. He was good, his omelette? Almost perfect! Our romance faded away when Sebastian left for Australia.

Then there was Andreas, the first proper cook I introduced to my family. (He was later to become top chef for a world-renowned hotel chain.) It was during my time with Andreas that the recurring pattern of me staying away from the kitchen finally broke, and I started to cook along with him, attempting bruschetta and tagliatelle, carrot cake, and tiramisus, steak tartare, and mille-feuille. I was slowly but steadily becoming a kitchen goddess, or so I thought…

My family seemed a bit happier, yet still unimpressed with Andreas. For them, cooking was not something you'd need to learn at college, it was something rather intangible, valuable, but never an astonishing accomplishment. Andreas dumped me after a year and a half. He made me scrambled eggs as I sobbed, heartbroken, on the day of our final goodbyes.

One Thomas and one George later, I tied the knot with Charlie, a doctor. He made me omelettes on every wedding anniversary. After twelve omelettes we divorced. I baked him a Tarte Tatin as a farewell gift, four and a half weeks ago.

I'm flying back home now. Single again. Hungry! Starving! It's early morning, and I'm sitting at the airport restaurant waiting for my flight. It's packed but I've managed to get a seat at a table in the corner, opposite a man glued to his laptop.

The waiter approaches and asks cheerfully, 'Ready to order?'

'Yes, please, an omelette,' we both reply.

Till Death Do Us Part

Whenever my mother tells me she had a dream seeing my grandmother, or my grandfather, my grandmother's sister, my father, or my nanny, then recounts in detail what they talked about, I don't think that she's out of her mind.

I only become slightly more cautious. Sometimes I'm even angry, at *them,* for appearing in our dreams, and only just checking on us, not saying anything expectedly wise, not telling us the stories from their otherworldly experiences. Isn't their mission to guide us through, spreading titbits of wisdom or any life-affirming messages around?

We've always lived together: Mom, Dad, my brother, me, my grandmother, and my nanny. There were two grandfathers I never met, because, sadly, they passed away long before I was born, but who nevertheless were always most actively present in our lives. 'Never met in person' would actually be more appropriate here. Their presence was strong through many photographs we had and lots of personal belongings. I remember my grandfather's compass and a stopwatch and a cigar case my father kept in his study, and brought out from time to time.

The 'till death do us part' concept never worked in our case, since it seemed we were not parted by death from our relatives. Those who passed away stayed with us, talked to us, came in our dreams, and occasionally gave advice. There were no ghostly stories, ghost whisperers, or psychic readings involved.

In our mundane, casual conversations, we'd mention our deceased family members as if they were still dining with us, or as if they were joining us in watching TV, discussing politics, gossiping, or solving word puzzles, just as my grandmother Maro did.

I can remember her voice only if I try really hard, if I shut the other voices out. Memories are overlapping as they resurface...

We're sitting on the backseat of the car, she's holding my hand, it's an evening, midweek, we're returning home, me from kindergarten, she from work. She's wearing a black skirt and a blouse, and a coat, very soft as I touch it. She's opening her bag and bringing my favourite candies out. I'm quickly unwrapping one and throwing it into my mouth. 'Careful,' she tells me, then unwraps another one and we're both delightfully chewing little mint candies on our way home, before dinner. You weren't allowed to eat anything before dinner, but that was our little secret.

I can see her silhouette, I remember her hair was grey, her eyes the colour of honey and almond. She taught me how to crochet and knit, and gave me my first books to read. I remember what she wore at home, a home robe, dark and velvety blue with tiny yellow flowers on it. She had a shiny black bag, commonly called a 'ridicule', and smoked cigarettes. I remember her smell, that perfume of hers, her fingers, how she sat at the table coming from work, surrounded by magazines, always choosing the ones with the most difficult word puzzles. That image never fades away...

Much later, I discovered she had lost two very young sons. It's because of her I have a sweet spot for old ladies smoking cigarettes. The scent of my childhood is of tangerines, black mulberry, green apples, sea, and Poison perfume by Christian Dior, and of Shalimar by Guerlain.

My older brother and my cousin were perfect at skiing, tree climbing, cycling, roller-skating, skateboarding, and ice cream eating without getting tonsillitis. I, on the other hand, was sure I would immediately get a bad throat if I'd get even one ice cream, or I'd immediately fall down from a mulberry tree if I even put my feet on it. The authority of my nanny, Dora, luring me out of those risky activities was unquestionable. As much as she loved all of the children in our family, she never bothered to hide that I was her darling. She saw her ultimate job as pushing me out of anything potentially dangerous that would harm me physically, so skateboards, bicycles, and roller skates were strictly banned. Much to her disappointment, my knees and elbows bled occasionally. 'Didn't I tell you, those silly things are not for you? You better go read,' she'd tell me, putting a greenish substance on my knee to disinfect the wound. It took me several summers and hundreds of unsuccessful attempts to finally figure out that rather than joining my brother's and my cousin's adventurous squad, it would be better to get rewarded with a plate full of delicious food.

As a child I often said I had five grandmothers. My schoolteachers only smiled in disbelief, thinking I was fantasizing, when in reality I wasn't. There was Lena, who was spending almost all of her free time with me, entertaining me, taking me out to the park attractions, and bringing me delicious hot pretzels she knew I adored. She made the best French fries I've ever eaten for dinner. She was blind in one eye and beautiful. She took me to the Easter mass for the first time in my life, and when I grew older she asked me to never marry a German man. I never married at all.

'Be careful, check electricity, check gas, check that the iron is switched off, before you leave,' was a refrain I heard most often. 'Be careful,' my two grandmothers told me, and I often found those precautions so annoying.

To my grandmother's sister Margot, I was a visiting grand-daughter. 'Are you my Nina, or Manana's Nina?' she'd ask whenever I called. Her Nina was my cousin who was raised by her, lived with her, and was an unmovable number one, steadily holding the rank of her beloved grandchild. Margot, who never had her own children, raised my mother, my aunt, and my uncle, had a sharp tongue, was a magician of a cook, loved football, and possessed a unique set of matchmaking skills that she wanted to sometimes try on me.

'Turn the TV on, he's there, he seems so intelligent and his mother would die for you to meet him sometime,' she'd call, hanging up after hearing my hysterical laughter in return.

'Be careful' boomerangs at me, and it's only now that I realise what it meant. It meant that I had to be alert, to be prepared and ready. All of my grandmothers knew better, having had their fair share of dramas and tragedies, losing their loved ones, their husbands, and their children. Probably they wanted me to know that apart from 'happily ever afters' there were great love stories, tragic losses and pain, and there were stories of survival and persistence. They probably wanted me to be aware that 'happily ever afters' were in fact exceptions, and if I didn't get mine, I would at least have examples to rely on.

A huge portrait of my grandfather was hanging in my grand-mother's house; a very handsome man with a little moustache,

23

who tragically died after a gas explosion at home. Left with three children, my grandmother Nina never married again.

'Will you write about me, someday?' she asked me once.

Going to the cemetery on a New Year night, bringing candles, candies, and wine, was a family tradition she initiated in memory of her late husband, a ritual my father didn't much appreciate, wasn't particularly fond of, not to say detested, despite the fact that he adored his mother-in-law.

For my father, with all of his joie de vivre, New Year was not exactly the right time for visiting those who had passed away, even if they were your closest family members.

For my dad, New Year was the celebration of life at its fullest, the one time when you could legitimately leave your deceased family members alone. He found it odd, and never joined my mother during those rounds. It was a clash of life philosophies, the one thing he would never agree on. I usually preferred to stay with him, and we sipped wine, seated at the New Year's table, while my mom, my aunt, and my uncle went to salute my deceased grandparents and wish them a happy year ahead. We saluted them too, but always chose to stay home.

My cousin recently confessed that she's team my father too. As for me, I'm in between, carefully considering. *Carefully* being a keyword here.

A Letter to My Unborn Children

I bet you didn't want to live by the park, which for your information is now being renovated, and in today's world, with global warming and climate change at the top of the world agenda, I'd consider myself lucky for a chance to be pushed in a stroller towards the park on a daily basis, where there still is some green space miraculously untouched. And by the way, that same park is the exact place where I, your mother, was hit by a sudden musing to write a book, which never got to a best-sellers list, and hardly anyone outside my circle of family and close friends have read or heard of it, but never mind. We're not here to talk about my questionable achievements.

What I can wholeheartedly understand, though, is that you don't want to live in the central part of the city, the so called prestigious neighbourhood, right? Well, maybe you have a point, considering a bunch of very uncool neighbours around, and a group of construction workers from the apartment building across the road, which, I'm afraid to say, know every stripe on all of my pyjamas by heart. Yes, I don't need you reminding me that my collection of lingerie and nightwear is infantile, as are my slippers. I'd refer to your prospective grandmother for that.

I assume you have decided in favour of some other woman, with a successful career, mind-blowing salary, and blond highlights. Someone working in marketing for sure—oh, those glossy, glamorous types! Did I guess it right? I know what's on your minds, kids! That yoga-aficionado marketing executive over there, with a short bob, hurrying to her car after the morning workout, holding a cup of coffee in one hand and scrolling her social media accounts with the other, deciding where to post an after-workout selfie, carefully choosing from which particular angle to capture and expose her freshly botoxed lips and a solarium-tortured body. I respect your decision to not be brought into this world by me, giving for starters that I'm not the queen of packing or unpacking suitcases, a very important skill, by the way. I'm so proud you're such a smart duo! Of course, we would need someone else to prepare you for wherever you'd be going; a summer camp or a winter resort. True, packing is not my strongest asset, nor is cooking, sewing, crocheting, driving, drawing, cleaning the house, or taking care of plants. Also, I'm terrible at math, have zero sense of orientation in space, no matter whether unknown or familiar; I'm a coffee and cigarette addict, and when I was a teenager I had terrible acne, so if you were mine, my loves, you'd probably have it too. Also, I often have migraine, so be aware, you might inherit that as well.

Oh, and you should see my belly! Listen, jump at any chance of visiting the Louvre Museum, in Paris, France, and when you see one of Titian's or Rubens's paintings, you'll instantly understand what I'm talking about. If I were you, I wouldn't recommend me as a travel companion, either. I'm a terrible—read, indecisive—shopper. If you don't believe me, here's my friend Margot, for reference. Oh, yeah, she'll have some stories for you to tell, not the lullaby types, I warn you. Don't even think of asking any other of my girlfriends—say, Helen, since the stories she has are the *Shining* type: frightening. If you have no idea what I'm talking about, I'd recommend you just forget and wait until you reach at least eighteen. Then, I guess, we could negotiate.

Sorry, I completely forgot to mention that I wear glasses. Right, yes, you wouldn't want to wear them since the age of nine months, as I did, I perfectly get it. However, if I were you, I wouldn't mind at all. I saw a beautiful collection of very expensive frames this summer, and I'd probably make you buy me one as a present for my eightieth birthday. You'd ask, why so late? Because I'm not a selfish egoist, you know! I would patiently wait till the day you became rich enough to buy them. See? I'm not that super-ambitious mom type.

Sorry, did I hear someone just say 'clumsy'? I have to admit, I am clumsy, and chances are those glasses would be broken in the very, very nearest future, so don't you bother buying them. And, speaking of buying, yes, maybe that summer house of mine is too small for you. You'd probably prefer a bigger one with a pool and a Jacuzzi and basketball and tennis courts? Well, if that's the case, I agree, it's rustic and shabby, and yes, I see dog hair on a couch. I don't mind mild shedding, you know.

I'm very sorry you're allergic to dogs. Thank you, I'm terribly aware you wouldn't want to share your home with pets and you'd want your mother marching in high heels, red lipstick on, not those comfy sneakers. Well, my darlings, let me disappoint you, I have a terrible habit of eating my lipstick off and heaving afterwards in most inappropriate places. If I were you, I wouldn't worry about it, just as I wouldn't worry about your late nights out, heavy hangovers, vibrant sex life (enough of condoms, agreed), idiot boyfriends, and somewhat hysterical girlfriends. I swear, I wouldn't at all worry about you leaving me empty-nested, dropping out of university, being fired, or quitting a third job in a row, and epically failing at new job interviews. I would not mind you not knowing how to make your bed, or how to wash your linens, or how to make savings. I wouldn't mind you leaving your husbands or wives for the new, all-consuming loves and an unidentified marital status; I would never worry about your salaries and promotions and jerk bosses and bitchy colleagues.

What I would worry about, however, is how hard you laugh. I would want to see you belly laughing, gasping for air, tears bursting out of your eyes laughing, inhaling and laughing again even harder, in a high-pitch, loud, 'I don't give a fuck whoever's around' laugh, the one only your mom could master.

A Belated Apology to My Dog

[2]'That's it,' Annika, the vet, told me after the second injection. I bent over, burying my face into your fur, inhaling your smell, stroking your fluffy, velvety ears. I didn't cry. 'Bye, see you...' I whispered, stood up, and left the room, still gripping your blue retractable leash. The other vet came in with a huge empty dog food bag and put your body inside, covered in a blanket, then zipped the bag up.

'I'll now call the burial service. It's forty lari, and I won't take anything for putting him down,' she said. I paid and gave her your leash. 'Give it to someone,' I told her.

'Yep, Figu was a happy dog, so let's give it to someone who might need it,' Annika agreed, and I left, into a sunny January afternoon.

My right hand still senses the grip of the leash, as if we're going for a walk, and I hold the leash tight to avoid car bumpers and tires on which you regularly peed, as if we're to avoid other dogs coming our way, because you, let's be honest, were never properly socialized, and never really liked other dogs. You sure preferred humans, your squishy orange ball, and my slippers.

Before meeting you, I didn't know what the hell 'blue roan' meant. All the cocker spaniels I've met or seen were either black or red coloured. But wait, no, that's not true. Many years ago, there was one particular dog I adored. He lived in Brno, Czechoslovakia, his owners our close family friends, and ever since I saw Akim, the black-and-white Cavalier King Charles Spaniel, I dreamed of having a dog. I had two dogs before you: Charlie, a poodle I had for two years in my teens, and then Jerry, a black English cocker spaniel who died in a dog fight when I was at a winter resort. Those deaths are too far from me now. I clearly remember, I cried. Why the hell am I not crying now?

My mind races back to the day when you ate that dead rat in the park, remember? And to the many days when you so gleefully rolled in those disgusting, stinky substances, looking so eternally happy, and the day when you ran off on the beach, and I ran after you in my swimsuit, screaming like a maniac. But you didn't care. You pretended to be deaf. You were the champion of pretending to be deaf. You didn't care whether it was a pouring rain, or a snow, or whether I was sleepy, or with a banging hangover! You simply adored waking me up. How very selfish of you! You'd sell your soul for a roasted chicken, or a disgusting fish head fresh out of a garbage can. A dead cat was among your most exquisite gourmet pleasures. When you got older, your mouth smelled of rotten fish. Sorry, but it's true.

I don't know if you were ever happy with me. I often came home late, and you waited. I didn't play with you as much as you'd want me to. I often left you with others for weeks when I travelled. We never went to a café or a restaurant together, because, frankly, there are not many dog-friendly places in this city. You never had proper sex, just innuendos and flirting, and I'm sorry for that. Luckily, you fell in love with Jiji the bulldog just for a day, remember? You never had puppies, I'm terribly sorry for that too. I'm sorry for not taking you to the park for one last time, and I'm sorry for not taking you to Paris at least once. You deserved a nice, long walk in the Luxembourg garden.

You were not my dog; you were me. The best me, the most mischievous me, the happy me, the 'life is good' me, the 'what the heck, let's have fun' me, the 'carpe diem' me, the sad me, the cuddly me, the neurotic and scared me.

I should have kept that leash. I'm an idiot, and you know it better than anyone, don't you?

Dembe

'You will have a black Lab,' my father told me last winter, rather imperatively. There were three of us standing in a tight circle: me, my dad, and Maya. I had nothing against black Labs, or any dogs of any colour, except that my dad passed away some eleven years ago, and seeing him in a dream took me by surprise. Why would he bother mentioning black Labradors stunned me even more.

'I saw Dad yesterday,' I told my mother over breakfast the next morning, hoping she'd have something to say. It seemed she wasn't too impressed, tired of my dreams ever since we'd lost our dog.

'That's great, it can mean you'll have someone to protect you,' she only said and left for work, leaving me with the vague explanation. As long as there was nothing of a threat in my dad's message, she was okay with it.

I continued drinking my coffee, the no-dog period in my life getting me used to the laziness of calm, enjoyable mornings, versus the frenzy of wake-ups and dog walks, versus the rush, when you're not fully awake, and don't have time to wash your face properly, let alone take a shower. Owning a dog means skipping morning shower, as well as breakfast and other necessary routines normal people do. The only thing that matters is your dog struggling not to pee inside, while you're putting your jacket on, simultaneously checking yourself in the mirror and not recognizing yourself. That woman with an awful hair, sleepy face, and wearing shapeless jeans can't be me!

I'm different now! My hair is perfectly coloured and styled, and my manicure is shiny and immaculate, and my skin is radiant! That's how I look, and I catch myself thinking that the transition from a dog-owner to a non-dog-owner might be timely, and liberating, and just a tiny bit sad, and I wipe that last thought off my mind, because I'm now bravely marching into a new stage of my life without a dog and I vow not to get sentimental. No more dogs. No more vet visits, no more rotten rats eaten, no more rolls in disgusting substances, no more frantic searches for dog sitters, no more unanswered annoying questions on when am I going to finally start a family of my own instead of obsessively caring for my dog! No more guilt for leaving my dog and travelling abroad.

But just when I'm crystal clear and thrilled about my new life path and the many adventures a non-dog-owning life is going to bring me, Maya calls, excited, asking if I'm home, and from the tone of her voice I already know she's up to something and is dying to share it with me.

'It's decided, and I need your help, but first, put the kettle on, let's have a coffee,' Maya almost screams into my ear, and in about fifteen minutes she's at my doorstep gleaming with joy.

I have no idea what's on her beautiful mind.

'I'm getting a dog!' she announces. 'Let it be a yellow Labrador! Labs are so affectionate! No, let it be an Akita! They are gorgeous, strong, and clever! They project dignity! Oh, what about German shepherds? Aren't they the best?' She's bubbling with excitement.

I can see it is hard for her to decide, and she's waiting for my approval.

For Maya, I'm a walking Animal Planet encyclopedia, or maybe even a dog whisperer. She wholeheartedly acknowledges that one expertise of mine. But I didn't want the joy of my friend becoming a dog owner to blind us. Is she ready for a dog? A large dog, which sheds, often drools and poops, and pees and chews everything around? It's not about Maya alone. It's about her family. Do they really need one? Maya is a busy mom of two, and getting a dog would only add many more responsibilities to her. In fact, she's going to have a third child, a furry one.

'Maya, listen, slow down for a second, it's not that easy,' I start, trying to bring as much authority to my voice as possible. 'Dogs are difficult to handle, your dog will need baths and toys and vaccination and constant attention, and when it gets ill, you get crazy, and then it gets old and it dies, and it's gonna be heartbreaking for you and the kids, and...' I'm reading a 'never get a dog' manual from out of my head as I created it.

'I know, but I'm the readiest I can be, so stop talking me out of it, will you? Please, just help me find a kennel, then we'll go see the puppy, don't you want to cuddle a puppy?' she says pleadingly, and before she finishes the sentence, I know there's no going back.

'A Lab it is!' I exhale and wink. 'You'll have the best puppy, I promise,' I tell her, and that same evening, she's already calling a kennel we found on Facebook.

Maya is determined to see a puppy the next day and to bring me with her. I still have my doubts. I can't quite understand why she is so willing to bring more unnecessary burden and headache into her life. Why now?

'They said they had one six-month-old puppy left from a

previous litter, and he's not yellow, he's brown, so we'll just go and see, okay? I'm more into the yellow ones, you know,' Maya tells me hurriedly, leaving no time for arguing.

'What did you just say?' I ask.

'Yep, he's not yellow. He's brown, only one left, a boy. Are you okay? Are you having flashes?' Maya looks at me puzzled.

'I'm fine,' I lie. I can very well feel the hair rising on my neck and droplets of sweat on my forehead.

'Oh, look, there they are!' She stops the car at the parking lot abruptly.

A man is walking towards us with a brown puppy on a leash. I have never seen a dog as beautiful and as sad as that one. His brown eyes so deep, he surely already knows what is ahead for all of us, and doesn't really care about it. That indifference strikes me. That puppy gives an impression like he spent all of his life in a Buddhist monastery.

I don't quite remember what the breeder talked about, while we stood there in the street. Neither Maya nor I could take our eyes off the dog that still had no name.

'I can't decide right away, I'll need to think it over, I'll call you tomorrow,' Maya finally says to the breeder, and I look at her in shock. What the hell is she doing? She is ruining all the magic!

'Can I have a word with you for a second?' I touch her arm slightly then whisper, 'Listen, you need to absolutely take him today, now! I know this dog was meant to be yours.'

'How the hell do you know? Didn't you tell me yesterday that it's hard, and they age, and they die, and all that shit?' She hushes and stares at me suspiciously.

'Well, yes, but forget it, it's all crap. I...I had a dream.' I look at Maya straight.

'Hah?' Maya seemed even more bewildered. I'm telling her

about my dad, and us, and him saying that I was going to have a black Lab. The good thing about friends is that they do not immediately think you've lost your mind, they give you some time and credit. Maya listens to me very carefully, and says after a long pause: 'But he's brown, not black, and it's me who's going to have that pup, not you...'

'Well. I'm sure Dad messed something up with colours and ownership, it doesn't matter, the message is clear though. Maybe there are no colours at all there...you know...' I try to reassure and convince her.

'Aha, you and your dreams, and philosophies.' She sighs, and turns to the puppy owner smiling.

'Okay, I'm taking him.' Maya pays for the dog, and we help the puppy climb into the car.

'I will name him Dembe, as one of the characters from *The Blacklist*,' she tells me when we are approaching her house.

'Sounds great, but I'd rather call him Einstein, he sure knows a secret or two,' I reply, and pet Dembe, who is already snoring in my lap.

In several years, he might be bred, and maybe I'll have a black Labrador then, I think to myself, pressing my nose to the car window, smelling the beginning of spring in the air.

Ara Means No! Or, the Art of Saying No

I
t didn't happen all at once. I've realised the strength, the power, the beauty, and the magic of the word 'no' (Ara) in Georgian only just recently, but as the saying goes, better late than never. And while I'm still mastering the craft of saying a big, fat, ugly NO, here's what I came up with in the process.

No is for not loving and appreciating yourself without feeling guilty, or without thinking you are a self-centred narcissist;

No is for not doing something you're not into doing. **No** is a yes, to staying home, reading books, binge-watching the TV shows you've missed, writing, and not going out with friends, even if they worry you're becoming antisocial. **No** is for not valuing and treasuring your time, spending it in whichever way you feel appropriate, even if it seems weird and odd to others;

No is for listening to someone's dramas, melodramas, or psychological thrillers, giving them advice on how to overcome crisis. You're not a crisis manager, nor are you a shrink;

No is for not leaving any event if you're bored to death and feel uncomfortable;

No is for not speaking your mind, even if everyone else thinks otherwise;

No is for sacrificing yourself to others and worrying about being an egoist;

No is for ignoring people who question your abilities, without being afraid to sound rude;

No is for torturing yourself, for being an imperfect daughter, sister, or friend;

No is for those with a super-competent tone, who never ever doubt their decisions and choices;

No is for the ones taking themselves too seriously;

No is for the ones thinking you're only accomplished if you're married, with children, or if you have a great career;

No is for the perfectionists who never failed;

No is for those who characterise you as sweet;

No is for not saying no, screaming it out loud and clear from the top of your lungs if and whenever necessary;

And finally, *No* is for the ones who don't like chocolate!

Do You Speak English?

I do. If asking a flight attendant to switch off the air conditioning with no tangible result counts, then yes, I surely do speak English. If not getting a single word from a taxi driver, bank accountant, and a waiter in New York counts, then, yes, again. If standing in front of a receptionist in a hotel in London and nodding to him maniacally, hiding the fact that you're struggling to catch what he's saying, counts as comprehending the verbal exchange, then yes, I do. If saying your own name with the best British accent you're able to master is the only thing you're mumbling counts, then yes, yes, and yes.

One of the most complicated, turbulent, exhausting, and rewarding experiences I've had in my entire life is with the English language, bringing the most joyous, fulfilling, funny, and embarrassing moments I can remember.

Munich, Germany, beginning of the '90s:

I'm a jury member of a short-film student festival, which means I'm watching zillions of movies from all over the world every day, discussing them afterwards with the fellow jury members.

During the screening of one of the Georgian shorts, it appears the film has no English subtitles and I'm assigned to provide a simultaneous translation, which I do, what seems to me now purely thanks to a high adrenaline flow. The film gets the festival prize for the best original screenplay several days later.

Lesson learned: Improvisation is the key!

Derby, UK, 1999:

I'm in a train taking me to Derby, where I'm to spend one month for cultural events management training. It's there in the train car I discover that Derby is pronounced as 'dhaabi', and for the first time, I start to seriously doubt whether the language I've been learning practically all of the conscious part of my life was English at all. Wasn't my teacher telling my parents I had a good ear for languages? Excuse me, which languages exactly?

I turn out to be incapable of hearing the name of that city without jumping from my seat every three minutes, afraid to fall asleep, and asking if we're in Derby yet, and when a kind stranger tells me, 'No, not yet there, luv,' my language-earnest ear only catches a No, while the rest of the sentence vanishes in the air, as too many other things evaporate from my mind during my stay in the UK that year. First, all of the English grammar disappears, then, even as I try to remember what were the books I read during my English lessons, I can't think of anything but *The Count of Monte Cristo* and *The Three Musketeers*. *Jane Eyre*, 'Rip Van Winkle', *Captain Blood*, and *David Copperfield* are gone and forgotten. It turns out I was a Francophile who had infiltrated an English terrain.

I only started slowly communicating, expressing myself and understanding what others were telling me, towards the end of my fellowship; and by the time I was able to build a coherent sentence or two, one month had flown by, and I was already returning to Tbilisi.

Lesson learned: When completely lost in translation, you can still learn to dance the rumba with a stunningly handsome dance teacher.

Leicester, UK 2004–2006:

Armed with the experience of working endless translations, long correspondences, seminars, conferences, and trainings, I'm deciding that this is the time to study more, and apply to the master's degree program at one of the universities in the UK. I'm all confidence, looking forward and ready to learn, absorb the knowledge I'll be acquiring, willing to dive into all the information the excellent tutors will be providing. I'm ready to draft essays, and read books, and listen to lectures, and actively engage in discussions. All of it is true. Except I have never rewritten, resubmitted, or edited my work for so many times, I've never felt with such intensity that I know absolutely nothing! The two years of the program were the most demanding, hard, challenging, the most satisfying and fun.

Lesson learned: Your work may be bad, but not disastrous.

Tbilisi, Georgia 2013–2015

I write a book, and then...I translate it into English. The 'then' consisting of a 532-pages-long agony, encouragement, discouragement, hyphenations, characters' points of view, dialogues, settings, edits, through which I occasionally want to kill, not a mockingbird, no, but some of my characters, myself, or my editors.

This is where this story actually ends, and if you're reading this essay, it probably means that a new book is either published or is under way.

   Lessons learned: ...

Note: No editor was harmed during writing and editing of this book.

Notes

MAKE ME AN OMELETTE

1   First published in an online journal Funny Pearls www.funnypearls.com

A BELATED APOLOGY TO MY DOG

2   First Published in an online literary magazine Virtual Zine www.virtu-
alzinemag.com

About the Author

Nino Gugunishvili is also the author of a women's fiction novel, *Friday Evening, Eight O'Clock*, published in English and Russian. She resides in Tbilisi, Georgia.

Also by Nino Gugunishvili

Friday Evening, Eight O' Clock
Tasha is a dreamer in search of a new dream. Shes bored with Pilates. Shes never tried yoga. She doesnt even have a drivers license. She lives a pretty ordinary life as a freelance writer who battles the occasional flow of melancholy with the regular flow of martinis. Nestled into her couch, her television remote in one hand and a cold adult beverage in the other, shes found a favorite way to pass the hours on a Friday evening. Its comfortable and familiar, but its not exactly an exciting way to live. With two of her closest friends, a bossy mother, an eighty-two-year-old grandmother, and Griffin, her fat yellow Labrador at her side, she knows that there has to be something better out there.

But where?

When she gets an unexpected offer to relocate to France to write a magazine column, she thinks her circumstances are improving. But life in a new country isn't all peches et la creme. Now far away from her comfort zone, Tasha must find the inner strength to start a new career and navigate the bizarre and unknown world of professional jealousy, intrigue, and conflicting personalities in a very foreign land.